DISTURBING THE LIGHT

JAMES BABBS
DISTURBING THE LIGHT

INTERIOR NOISE PRESS
Austin, TX

Disturbing the Light
Copyright © 2013 by James Babbs

All rights reserved. Printed in the United States of America. No part of this book may be used or reproduced in any manner whatsoever without written permission except in the case of brief quotations embodied in critical articles and reviews.

For order information and current mailing address please visit www.interiornoisepress.com

Interior Noise Press
Austin, TX

Cover Photo by Romina Olson
Book Design by David p Bates

Library of Congress Control Number: 2012951727

ISBN 978-09816606-7-7
First Edition

*to Candy with
all my love*

CONTENTS

Photograph: Early Seventies	15
Last Night at the Chinese Buffet	16
That's What Friends Are For	18
Last Day of the Year	21
Come Dancing	22
Hello Cowgirl in the Sand	23
Something Crazy	24
Disturbing the Light	25
Dream Where I Was a Blackbird	26
Lost Cause	27
Above Us	28
Going to the Zoo	29
Before the Shootings	30
Empty Bottles	31
Recovery & Loss	32
I Hate the Toilet Paper in Public Restrooms	33
Tonight I'm Drinking Trying to Forget You	34
Wrong Number	37
8 Birds on the Wire	38
What the Hell do I Know About Love	39
I Asked Her Out	40

Things That Aren't Important Happen All the Time	41
I Dream of Trees	43
Fat Kid Across the Street	44
What Happened to the Future	45
The Madman	46
Listening to My Father	47
Jack & Coke & Tonight's the Night	48
When I'm Drunk I Think She's Beautiful	49
I Just Wanted to Eat Breakfast	51
Apartment 2A	52
I've Been Thinking About Heartbreak	53
Counting the Red Ones	54
Does It Always Have to End in Sadness	56
Married With 3 Kids	58
I Asked Her What Name	59
First Day of Summer	60
Driving Around Thinking	61
This Morning in the Paper	62
Hardees, Monday Evening in December	63
Every Month My Father	64
Windmills at Night	65

Two Bottles of Cheap Wine	66
Wake-Up Call	67
My 8th Grade Year	73
We Laugh About It Now	74
I Felt the Waves Crashing Over Us	75
What I Saw	76
They Say	77
Meat Loaf Amen	78
Waiting Room	80
Monkey Pile	81
The Way She Says My Name	83
Better Than Yesterday	84
Black Spiral Notebook	85
In the Room Where We Hide	86
Getting Offers In the Mail for Gay Porn	87
Marissa	89
Dark Red Plastic	90
Where Babies Come From	91
The War on TV	93
Boys	94
This Morning I Remember My Father	95
Friday Night Fish Fry Down at the Legion Hall	96

It's Only a Paper Moon	97
Union 76 Truckstop, After 2am	99
Trying to Write My Own Love Song	100
He'll Feel It in the Morning	101
Getting Old	102
Everybody Needs a Dream	103
Pieces	104
The Phone Dials Your Number	106
Flashes of Light	107
Another Sunday Morning Hangover	108
I Keep Coming	109
Applebees, Cold Thursday Night	110
Plastic Cowboy	111
Because	112
Walking Home Drunk Again	113
Teacher	114
The Night My Brother Died	115
Light Comes Through the Window	116
This Morning Over the Phone	117
I Don't Know What I Want	118
The Neighbor's Daughter	119
I Wanted to Know Her Name	121
Cruel Summer	122

When I Speak Your Name	123
The Sound of His Voice	124
The Good Life	125
Sometimes I Wish I Could Do It Again	127
I Felt Her Body Shiver	129
Driving Home	131
How Often Do You See Them	132
The Tuba Player	133
Blue Toenails	134
Toward the End	136
The Sound of Machines	137
Peach Schnapps and Sprite	138
The Smell of Burning Leaves	139
Windmills In the Rain	141
First Time	142
The Boy with the Plastic Telephone	143
Two Sisters	144
Empty Chair	145

*Any thought that I have right now
isn't worth a shit because I'm totally
   fucked up*
                  Richard Brautigan

*early in the mornin'
at the break of day
he used to sleep
until the afternoon*

              Neil Young

Photograph: Early Seventies

you're gathering water
from the mountain spring
filling up plastic milk jugs
is it Kentucky
or is it Tennessee
I look at the photograph
without remembering
the actual event
but I must have been there
five or six years old
and that means you must
have been sixteen
maybe seventeen
wearing cut-offs made
from an old pair of jeans
yellow shirt screaming
the seventies every
time I see it
and you're smiling
as if you're just
happy to be there
death still far away
beyond the scope of
the camera's lurking eye

Last Night at the Chinese Buffet

I'm eating egg rolls with
hot mustard and sweet
and sour sauce when I hear
the guy a few tables over
getting belligerent with the waitress
I can tell he's been drinking
by the way he slurs his words
repeating himself and thrusting
his finger at her while his wife
sits meekly across from him
looking down at the table and
he keeps telling the waitress
he wants another beer and
by god she better get him one or
something I can't understand and
then the manager walks over or
at least I assume it's the manager and
he starts telling the guy to
please calm down and the wife
looks as if she's on
the verge of tears and
I just want to get up and
get some fried dumplings and
that soy sauce with the onions in it
but I'm afraid to move
because the man's screaming at
the manager with a barrage of
swear words and everybody
in the restaurant has stopped
eating and are all staring at the man
his wife's crying now
asking him to please quiet down and
I can tell she's had to
do this before in other places
pleading with him and hoping
but eventually settling for
a little less and suddenly

I'm no longer hungry but
an hour from now
who knows

That's What Friends Are For

couple of days ago I decided
I'd go around to my buddy's house
because
I hadn't heard anything from him
for the last two or three weeks and
I was starting to think
maybe something was wrong
I pounded on the front door
then I tried the knob
but it was locked
I went to the back of the house
walking through the unmowed grass
I tried the back door
but didn't have any luck
there was a basement window
on that side of the house
so I bent down and looked inside
I saw my buddy in the laundry room
standing about waist-deep in a hole
that had been broken in the floor
he was shoveling dirt and
putting it on the pile next to him
there were empty beer bottles
strewn around him and
fast-food wrappers and
dirty paper plates and
pieces of concrete
I beat on the glass and watched him jump
then he saw me and grinned
a couple of minutes later
he came to the door
what the hell are you doing
I asked
he was dirty and
covered in sweat and
he smelled like stale beer
listen, man

he said
his voice frantic
I'm really busy right now
what's going on
I said and
he motioned me down to the basement
he had this crazy look in his eyes
crazier than normal and
he hurried over to the corner
where papers were scattered and
started foraging through them
until he found the ones he wanted
here
he said
thrusting them at me
I took them from him
glancing at the top one
not really sure about
what I was suppose to see
he said
I'm digging a bunker
a place to hide
you know what I mean
I said
okay
you don't get it, man
he said
looking toward the laundry room
things are happening
he said
what kinds of things
I asked
he blew air out of his mouth and
I could smell his breath
it's all over the internet
he said and
I'm already way behind

I asked him
if he had any beer
check the fridge
he said and
he went back to work
I found two bottle on the top shelf
I took one and started drinking it
my buddy was back in the hole
shoveling out the dirt as fast as he could
they're going to start rounding people up
he said
I took a long drink
when's all this suppose to happen
I asked
soon
he said without stopping
I finished the beer
went back to the fridge and
started on the last one
I stood there without saying anything
I watched him for a couple of minutes
then I told him
I had to get going
but I said
I'd come back later on and
check on him and
could he give me some money
so I could run by the store
because
he was all out of beer

Last Day of the Year

driving down this country road
I've been on it before
you invited me to your party
but I decided not to go
and on the radio
there's a dead man singing
asking the same question
he asks
every time he sings his song
and the answer keeps changing
tonight
the road seems longer
I thought there was a sign here
showing how many more miles to go
to reach the next town
but I guess I was wrong

Come Dancing

I told her
I really don't think
I can do this anymore and
she didn't say anything
for the longest time
sitting there next to me
without the light on
I watched the darkness from outside
come dancing slowly across the room
finally I said
I'll always want more
than you do
she said
yes
you're right
but so softly
it was almost as if
she said nothing at all
I turned
trying to look out the window
but there was
nothing out there to see

Hello Cowgirl in the Sand

hello
cowgirl in the sand
can you tell me
how long has it been
somewhere
almost too far away
for me to remember now
the way we fell
into the sound of
our own breathing
long soft kisses and
the yearning
not to feel broken
anymore
the darkness
stretching over us
like some kind of new skin
sweet air
pouring into this room
after too many nights alone
Neil playing on the stereo
those long slow jams
our bodies touching
so real
it could've been a dream

Something Crazy

when it first happens
you feel like
doing something crazy
like calling her on the phone
then hanging up
whenever she answers
or hiding out
in front of her house
waiting for her to come home
but you just stay inside
getting drunk
every night for a week
when it's over
you emerge again into the light
start hanging out
with all your friends
laughing and joking
like you did before
but now you have
these long stretches of silence
where you stare off into nothing
and no matter what
anybody says
you never mention her name

Disturbing the Light

sitting here in
the living room watching
the way the sunlight falls
across the floor making
these rectangles of light and
I remember how you
always avoided them
whenever you got up to
go to the bathroom or
the kitchen stepping
carefully over them or
walking around them but
never just going through them and
one day I asked you
why you did this and
you laughed, softly
said you didn't want to
disturb the light and
now you're gone and
I want to run around the room
scream at the top of my lungs and
step into the middle of
all those rectangles so
the light shines on me and
no longer touches the floor

Dream Where I Was a Blackbird

before this there was fire and
something burned out of me
then rising from the ashes
my arms beating the air
I started soaring over rooftops
pulling in patterns the shingles
made with my sharpened eyes
before flying high above the trees
feeling the same way I always did
like I was inside my old body
but in my mind I knew and
when I opened my mouth
wanting to speak
the sound emerging made the people
turn their heads to look
hands held up before them
shielding their eyes from
the burning rays of the sun

Lost Cause

I started my drinking early
today
because staying sober
just doesn't seem to help
standing near the window
and it looks like rain
its looked this way
for hours now
but the ground's still dry
and there's very little wind
and the sun keeps making
these feeble attempts to
break through the clouds
and shine
but in the end
it's another lost cause
because the clouds keep gathering
they never give up
trying to smother the light
I turn away from the window
and walk into the kitchen
start looking in the refrigerator
just hoping for one more beer

Above Us

there were 3 girls that year
living in the apartment above us
two skinny blondes and
a tall dark brunette
we never spoke to them
just saw them
coming and going and
we heard them sometimes
up there moving around
we thought about them
wondered what they were doing
those nights
when we weren't doing anything
but sitting around and
we wondered what they thought
when we played the stereo loud
but they never complained
at least not
as far as we knew
one night
when we were having a party
we wrote an invitation
on a piece of notebook paper and
slipped it under their door
but we never heard from them and
the next morning
when I saw them leaving
they were laughing
talking about something
while slowly crossing the street

Going to the Zoo

I was thinking about
going to the zoo
but I didn't want to go alone
imagining those young mothers
holding their children close
watching me
whenever I walked by and
why does it make me feel guilty
when I know
I've done nothing wrong and
I like watching the sea lions
standing near the rail
for hours at a time
while they swim circles
around the pool performing
for the people and
maybe
it's just me
but they always look happy
not like the lions and
the tigers I see
pacing back and forth across
their cages looking restless and
I know how it feels
like you're trapped all the time
with nowhere to go and
it's probably too late
anyway
I mean
if they set them free now
after all these years
I'm pretty sure
they wouldn't want to leave

Before The Shootings

years before Columbine
Steve took me to the school parking lot
and showed me the gun he kept
under the seat of his truck
let me hold it in my hand
it was heavier than I expected
Steve said it was a three fifty-seven magnum
capable of blowing a hole the size of
a nickel through an engine block
I gave it back to him
and never considered him a threat
he put the gun back under the seat
and we went back inside

Empty Bottles

strewn over
a secluded gravel road
reminds me of the past and
I can hear the music
Dark Side of the Moon
Pink Floyd on 8-track tape
blaring from shitty speakers
all the windows rolled down
in Doug's gray-primered Pontiac
one of the girls asks him
if he has something
she can dance to
but Doug just laughs
says he doesn't listen to
any of that disco crap
she climbs up on the hood and
starts shaking what she's got
her body swaying to
the sound of *Money*
future vice-president of
our local bank branch and
still to this day
an attractive-looking
divorced mother of two

Recovery & Loss

woke up with the blues
this morning on the radio
balanced on the folding chair
right next to the bed
I've been sleeping in
my mother's apartment
while she's in the hospital
doing rehab
trying to recover from a fall
and the sun was warm
hitting me in the face
and when I looked at the clock
it wasn't as late as I thought
last night I kept dreaming
there was something chasing me
through the dark streets
of some unknown town
and I kept running
past the houses and the buildings
but I didn't recognize anything
at one point I stumbled into this bar
at the end of a dead-end street
and I felt all these strangers
staring at me with fear
swimming in their eyes
and I started asking them
about the address of my childhood home
but no matter
how many times I told them
none of them knew where it was

I Hate the Toilet Paper in Public Restrooms

I hate the toilet paper
they put in public restrooms
because
it's always way too thin and
why the hell do they have to
make it so narrow
so it'll fit in the holder
I guess
but why couldn't they
make the holder
a little bit larger
so the paper could be
a more normal size
and this is just one of the reasons
why I try to avoid using
public restrooms all together
but sometimes I can't help it
because
situations arise and
when they do
I make sure to
check the stall first
because
I want to know
before I sit down
if there's enough paper
and then
when I'm done
I have to go through
this whole process of
pulling the paper out
and straightening it
then folding it back together
until it's ready for me to use
having to do this
maybe
four or five times
my pants down around my ankles

Tonight I'm Drinking Trying to Forget You

1.
tonight
I'm drinking
trying to forget you
the bartender
this cute blonde
with the beautiful smile
bringing me another beer
and telling me how every night
she makes enough in tips to pay
her utilities for the month
she loves this job
but she's going to school
because
she wants to be a teacher
wants to work with kids
she has a son of her own
he just turned five and
looks like his father
but don't ask her about him
she hasn't heard anything
from him for a long time and
she doesn't know where he's at
doesn't really care
because
he's an asshole
and I watch the way she moves
like a dancer
I tell her
slurring my words a little
she'll own this place
before all's said and done
and she throws back her head
laughing with her eyes closed
and I think
oh hell
there goes another five bucks

2.
tonight
I'm drinking
trying to forget you
two guys across the bar
comparing tattoos
lifting their shirts and
turning around
so people can get a better view
when one of them
starts taking off his pants
somebody laughs
but his wife or girlfriend
or whoever she might be
slaps him and
tells him to stop
they start talking about their scars
the first guy saying
he got this one outside
some nightclub in Detroit
after some fat ass
mouthed off to his girlfriend
then the chickenshit
pulled a knife on him
instead of standing there
and fighting him like a man
the second guy saying
he got this one
when he was a kid
when he ran across the yard
and fell on a rake
and had to have fourteen stitches
and didn't have to go to school
for two or three days
and he laughs
talking about how mad his brother got
because
he didn't get to stay home

3.
tonight
I'm drinking
trying to forget you
but I keep thinking about you
wondering where you are
what you might be doing
tonight
while two attractive women
slow dance together
to a Van Morrison song
running their hands
over each other's bodies
and I see them
laughing
one of them touching
the other one's hair
telling the bartender
I need another beer
laying my money down
before I go to take a piss
walking past the guys
with the tattoos and the scars
wondering if I should tell them
about my own scars
the ones hidden on the inside
I can feel them in there
but I can't take my shirt off
and show them how they look
because
there's nothing for them to see

Wrong Number

today
when I get home
there are three missed calls
on my phone and
two messages flashing
on my answering machine
the calls are all from the same number
each one of them
about five minutes apart
the caller ID doesn't give a name
but I know they're from a cell phone
by the way they're listed
when I listen to the messages
one of them's just the sound of
a phone hanging up and
the other one's a man's voice
pleading to call him back
later
when the phone rings and
it's the same number
I decide
I want to answer it
is Linda there
he asks and
when I tell him no
meaning
no one by that name lives here
his voice sounds hollow
Oh
he says, then
sorry
I guess
I have the wrong number

8 Birds on the Wire

out behind my house
I see them
when I'm drinking my coffee
watching bird number six
move away from seven
and scoot closer to number five
then number five flies away
and bird number six waits
then moves back over to seven
they stay that way
for a little while
then both seven and eight
fly off together
I freshen up
my cup of coffee
the morning full of
fog and rain

What the Hell do I Know About Love

I've been wearing the same pair of socks
for the past three days and
I haven't bothered to shave
for over a week now
but it doesn't matter
because
I never go anywhere
I just stay at home
shuffling from room to room
it's after five o'clock and
I haven't started drinking yet
maybe
I should open a bottle of wine
or mix myself a tall glass
of whiskey and Coke
I realize
the world's filled with
beautiful women and
I don't know
what any of them want

I Asked Her Out

I wanted to take her
out to eat and
get to know her better
because
I thought
she was beautiful and
I couldn't stop
thinking about her
I remember
the first time we met and
how strange I felt inside
full of warmth and light
walking around
like I was a different person and
I wanted to ask her out
but I kept waiting
for just the right time
I wanted to make her laugh
because
I remember
she had this
incredible smile and
this way of looking at me
words could never describe
I remember
it was a warm afternoon and
we were alone together
of course
she looked just as
beautiful as ever and
everything felt right
so I walked up to her and
I asked her out
but when I did
she just looked at me
but she never smiled
then she kind of laughed
before she told me
no

Things That Aren't Important Happen All the Time

stopping at the gas station
on my way home from work
filling up the car and
maybe while I'm here
I'll get something to eat
they've got good subs
that they make themselves
so I head toward the kitchen
the woman at the front counter
where they keep the cigarettes and
the lottery machine
smiles at me
when she thinks I'm not looking
while I'm waiting for the girl
with braces on her teeth
to finish making my sandwich
I'm getting the classic combo
with ham and turkey and
roast beef and
she doesn't know Paul Newman
she says
the face on the salad dressing
reminds her of Maury
she says
you know
that guy with the talk show
I tell her
yeah
I know who he is
but that's Paul Newman on the bottle
he was an actor
I tell her
but I guess she's too young and
I start thinking of some of his movies
but I'm convinced
all the ones I come up with
she's not going to know

then I say
what about Tom Cruise and
The Color of Money
but she just frowns at me and
shakes her pretty little head and
I realize
even that one was made
long before she was born

I Dream of Trees

I've fallen through the cracks
where I have to look up
if I want to see the light
but it's warm here
and most days are dry
and softness covers
everything
the gentle dust of time
at night when I'm drunk
I brush my fingers over the walls
and think about skin
memories of your body
sweetness lingering
the bitter aftertaste
when I fall asleep
I dream of trees
the wind blowing
limbs bending
the horrible sounds they make
scraping against the house

Fat Kid Across the Street

I start watching
the fat kid across the street
pushing this wheelbarrow
loaded with dirt
down the sidewalk and
I don't know where he's going
but I see him lose the balance
the load shifting to one side
pulling the wheelbarrow with it
dirt spilling all over the walk
and I watch him
the look of exasperation
all over his face
before he struggles to
right the wheelbarrow again
disappearing for several minutes
returning with the shovel
putting the dirt back in place
standing there
admiring his work for a moment
wiping his hands on
the front of his shirt
starting again
walking slower this time
the sweat on his face
softly glistening

What Happened to the Future

we watched films about it
when we were at school
they told us
we were going to have
heated roads to melt the ice and snow
air-conditioned highways
running through the deserts and
cars that could drive themselves
while the family sat in the back
playing games together and
we were going to discover
how to grow food in those deserts
build farms beneath the oceans and
live in cities on the moon
nobody would ever go to bed hungry
nobody would ever die
from any horrible diseases and
there wouldn't be any more wars
we'd all have our own personal jet-packs
strapped to our backs
lifting us into the skies and
everyone would be free
with the wind blowing
into their faces and
loneliness
despair
would be something make-believe
that we'd watch for entertainment
on our giant TV screens

The Madman

on the corner
keeps screaming about
the government
how they're controlling
our weather and
last week it was
something about alien bodies
the recovery of UFOs and
there are meetings
being held in secret rooms and
I think
what if just once
something he said
turned out to be true
then there's still a chance
no matter how much
you protest
that you could love me too

Listening to My Father

it probably seemed like
I wasn't listening at all
but years later I'm standing in
the garage sharpening the blade
for the lawnmower and
his voice comes through
loud and clear
it's only the ends of
the blade that do the cutting
you only need to
sharpen the ends and
that's what I'm doing
using the same sander he used
grinding the ends until
they're shiny and thin
thinking of him
carefully looking it over
turning the blade slowly
in his hands before
nodding his head and
smiling at me
for a job well done

Jack & Coke & Tonight's the Night

the way Neil's voice sounds
almost broken and
I've felt that way
countless times before
at the end of another week
another jack and coke but
who's counting, right, and
I start thinking about you
how its been a long time
since I heard your voice and
I no longer remember
the sound of your laughter
and sometimes years feel as
fast as days passing and
things are always
closer than they appear
the music like the sound of
desperation
wafting through the darkness and
Neil climbs the ladder
with his head in the clouds
I get a little drunker and
sometimes it's enough

When I'm Drunk I Think She's Beautiful

Connie's behind the bar
tonight
where she's been for the past
35 years or so
serving up drinks and
trying to keep everybody in line
I'm one of her regulars
so she comes over and
talks to me
whenever she gets the chance
sometimes
I flirt with her
making her laugh
she tells me
she's old enough to be my mother
but when I'm drunk
I think she's beautiful and
I tell her
I want to marry her
I tell her
I want to live with her
right here in the bar
she comes back with
I just want her
for all the free booze
but I tell her
my voice louder this time
no
it's not true
I tell her
I love her and
every time I say it
she just laughs
on one of my better nights
when I end up leaving
with some other woman
turning back one last time

toward the bar
I don't know
maybe
it's just me
or the lighting
or something
but I swear
Connie always looks sad
when I tell her goodbye

I Just Wanted to Eat Breakfast

I wanted to eat breakfast
at Steak n Shake this morning
the one over there off of market street
because
I was going to Wal-Mart
when I finished
but when I got to the restaurant
it was closed and
I wondered
how long it had been
since Steak n Shake stopped
being open 24 hours
I noticed on the door
where it listed the hours
they now closed
every night at one a.m.
it was seven-thirty
on a sunday morning and
the sign said
they didn't open until ten
shit
I just wanted to eat breakfast
so I drove over to the Bob Evans
located down on the corner
I'd never been there before
but I ordered the Homestead breakfast
and sat there alone
drinking my coffee black
while contemplating
what the world was coming to

Apartment 2A

I was looking for
Millicent's apartment
the woman I'd been out with
a couple of times before
but I'd never been to her place
I didn't see her name on
any of the mailboxes and
I couldn't remember
what she'd told me
either 2A or 3A
but I didn't know which one
so I knocked on 2A and
she answered the door
maybe 19 or
20 years old and
she was wearing a black robe
her feet bare and
she had really cute feet
her toenails painted pink
I looked at her face and
it was only for a moment
but I wanted to kiss her
I wanted her to kiss me
she smelled really good and
she made me think of
flowers and
the warmth of the sun
I told her I was sorry
I had the wrong apartment and
she smiled at me
said no problem
in a soft voice
then she closed the door and
I walked back down the hall
lingered for a moment
near the bottom of the stairs

I've Been Thinking About Heartbreak

I've been drinking since I got home and
it's almost dark outside
I hear the barking
in the distance and
think it could be coyotes
running through the timber
and not just the sound
of the neighborhood dogs
something in the air
tonight
and I can't sit down for too long
I keep wanting to get up
and walk around the room
I've been thinking about heart break
about rain falling in the afternoon
and I wonder what it's like
being married to someone
and having them around all the time
tonight
I feel kind of tired
from the weight I keep dragging around
and maybe I'm angry
for no good reason
for letting myself get too old

Counting the Red Ones

we were out in the yard
with our lawn chairs and
I had the cooler between us
filled with ice and beers
she was a blonde I'd met
a couple of weeks before
she was wearing cut-offs and
this little red halter-top
that wouldn't stay in place and
she had to keep adjusting it
we'd been drinking for awhile and
I could tell she was getting restless
I'm bored, she said, let's do something
we are doing something, I said
and I emptied another bottle
tossed it behind me in
the grass along with the others
you know what I mean, she said
I started another beer
oooh, she said, there goes a red car
I just love red cars
I got inspired
why don't you count them, I said
she seemed to brighten
okay, she said
she liked playing games
she got a pen and some paper
there's one, she said, marking it down
she adjusted the halter-top
I watched her and drank more beer
there's another one, she said
she jumped out of her chair
almost losing the halter-top completely
I just love red, she said
it is a nice color, I told her
I stared at the halter-top
as I finished another beer

oooh, she said, there goes another one
I didn't realize, she said
there were so many of them
she readjusted the halter-top
so her tits stuck straight out
I pulled the last beer from the cooler
taking small sips every now and then
making it last for as long as I could

Does It Always Have to End in Sadness

she said
after reading what I had written
handing back the pages
I'd given to her
what's wrong with that
I said
having another drink from
the bottle of beer in my hand
do you only want happy endings
I asked her
she said
sometimes
well
I said
life's not like that
she said
I know
but do you always have to
keep reminding us
I said
baby
I'm just trying to keep it real
feeling a little drunk
I kissed her
watching her eyes grow wide
she laughed
maybe
she said
you won't like the way this ends
I kissed her again
it was my turn to laugh
I said
but this is just part of the story
I finished off the beer
tossed aside the empty bottle
I told her
don't worry baby

the ending will come
soon enough
for all of us
kissing her again
sneaking my hand up
the inside of her shirt

Married With 3 Kids

I started buying her beers
after she'd been there for awhile
sitting at the end of the bar
I kept watching her reflection
the mirrored-wall behind the bar
showing me her face
above the bottles of booze
how she lit her cigarette
and held it in her hand
I waited
at the end of the night
she came over and thanked me
asked me why I had
bought her all those beers
I said why not
trying to be cute about it
before she started telling me
she was married
with 3 kids at home
and a husband who worked late
brushing my arm
lightly with her fingers
before pushing the hair
away from her face
thanking me again
I told her no problem
watching her walk away
said to myself
what the hell
it was the least I could do

I Asked Her What Name

she wanted me to use
when I wrote about this moment
we were lying in bed
next to each other
our bodies touching beneath the blankets
she said
I don't know
can't you just use my real name
I told her
of course
but I was trying to protect her innocence
laughing as I felt her hand
grabbing at me
how about Samantha
she said
I said
yeah
like from Bewitched
and I asked her
to twitch her nose
the way Samantha did on the show
when she was trying to cast a spell
she made several attempts
and didn't even come close
but she looked so cute
while she was doing it
I told her not to stop

First Day of Summer

she wore a sundress
covered with flowers
glided over and asked me
to buy her a drink
said her name was Summer
told me her parents
gave her that name because
she was conceived on
the solstice and
I couldn't stand to
look at her for very long
gazing at her was like
staring at the sun
but we laughed and
drank together until
she asked me to
take her back to my place
we had to walk and
it rained all the way home

Driving Around Thinking

I've gone past these same houses
countless times before
but they never look any different
everything here stays the same
only the names seem to change
and I should've stayed in college
should've finished my degree
maybe
I'd be somewhere else now
driving around some other town
listening to the blues on the radio
but maybe I wouldn't be
the same person I am now
I mean
everything I did back then
has made me who I am
right?
I don't know
if I'd be willing to
risk changing that
as another blues song starts up
and I think
that's just how I feel
sometimes
the second line echoing the first one
the guitar wailing somewhere in the dark

This Morning in the Paper

when I saw his obituary
the first thing I thought about
was him and his brother
getting into a fight
on the bus
one day after school
his brother holding him
grabbing him in a headlock
punching him
over and over again and
I remember the way
he came up out of the seat
his face all red and
looking like he was going to cry
but instead
just turning toward the window
without making a sound and
they haven't lived around here for years
he's somebody I never thought about
only a couple of years older than me

Hardees, Monday Evening in December

I can hear them talking
their voices rising up
from the kitchen
the place is nearly empty
just me
alone in my booth and
some another guy asleep
near the back wall
I just want to finish my coffee
before heading for home
and I hear the waitress asking
what's it called when two people
have been married
less than six months and
they want to split up
but don't want to get divorced
but nobody answers her
and all the time I'm thinking
annulment
it's called an annulment
and why the hell won't
somebody answer her
but no one ever does and
I wait for her to ask again
but she just lets the conversation
drift into something else and
I hear the other guy mumbling
something in his sleep before I
throw my cup away and leave

Every Month My Father

takes over $500 worth
of pills prescribed
by his doctor but
still feels like shit
sits in his chair all day
too weak to do much
of anything else
he's diabetic
and blind
and has congestive
heart failure
and now he has
to go on
dialysis so
they want to restrict
the amount of fluids
he drinks each day
and still
there's all those fucking pills
to take

Windmills At Night

I see red lights blinking
just to the north of
where I'm driving
eastbound on 136
twenty miles or so
outside of rantoul
bluegrass music
playing on the radio
thoughts of you keep
turning in my mind
the wind strong tonight
pushing against the car and
red lights keep blinking
like sleepy eyes awakening
red eyes gazing up
toward the sky wondering
is there something out there
or are we destined to
forever be alone

Two Bottles of Cheap Wine

I guess she came to
see me because
she was having trouble
with her husband and
I'd heard they'd been
having some problems and
after she sat down
she told me he had
moved out last night
I poured us each a
glass of cheap wine
I'd purchased from
the Super Wal-Mart
a few days before and
then she cried and
told me all about it
through two bottles worth

Wake-Up Call

when I first saw her she was crying
looking down at the cell phone in her hand
I kept thinking
what an attractive girl she was
the kind of woman that made you ache
just looking at her
but I hadn't fucked anybody in a long time
so that may have had something to do with it
I went over and asked her
if she needed some help
oh
she said looking up
seeing me for the first time
I don't know
she said looking me over
I wasn't anything to write home about
as far as looks went
but I wasn't the worst looking guy in the world
she said
my car died and I was
trying to call my parents
I told her
okay
she hesitated
like she was weighing something in her mind
but I didn't know what it was
finally she said
we don't really get along
my parents I mean
I've been trying to move out
I said
oh, I see
I pretended to look at
the watch I wasn't wearing
I said
look
I can give you a ride and

if you want to
you can stay at my place
until you get things figured out
she told me her name was Candy
I asked her if she'd like to get a drink first
before we went to get her things
she smiled and said
she could certainly use one
I decided to take her to
this little out-of-the-way place
on the outskirts of town
it was nice and quiet and
they made the drinks strong
I think everybody in there
wanted to fuck Candy
when we walked into the place
including the women
she was definitely a good-looking girl
a hell of a lot better than most of the women
I was usually able to attract
we had one drink
then two drinks and three drinks and
it was almost midnight
when I told Candy
maybe
we should go get her things
she kissed me
pushing her tongue into my mouth
she said
okay and
I heard her laugh
we got up and helped each other to the car
Candy kept trying to give me
the directions to her parents' house
but every time I followed them
she told me *this isn't it*
after about an hour of this
we made it to the right place

I parked on the street and
told her I'd wait in the car
Candy gave me a sloppy kiss
told me she wouldn't be very long
I looked at the house
saw some lights come on
I heard arguing and
about twenty minutes later
Candy came out carrying two suitcases
I got out and put them in the trunk
Candy said
I'll be right back
she disappeared into the house again
this time I didn't hear any arguing
I guess they had said
all they wanted to say
Candy came back to the car
we drove to my place
I carried the suitcases into the house
Candy pulled a wad of bills from her purse
she said
I stole my Mom's emergency fund
and laughed
she keeps it in the freezer
wrapped up in aluminum foil
she doesn't think anybody knows about it
I put an SOS pad in its place
and put the whole thing back in the freezer
Candy laughed again
won't she be surprised
I took Candy to my bedroom
showed her where she could put her stuff
I told her it was getting late and
I was really tired
Candy gave me another kiss
a long slow one
I got undressed and climbed into bed
Candy put some of her stuff away

I heard her in the bathroom
I must have fallen asleep
because
when I woke up the room was dark
I felt Candy breathing next to me
I looked at the clock
I'd been asleep for a couple of hours
I pushed up against Candy
she murmured something and
I went back to sleep
in the morning
Candy gave me a wake-up call
she started by sucking my cock
then she climbed on top of me and
rode me all the way to the end
we showered together
I took my time washing Candy's tits
I made sure they were nice and clean
I asked her what she wanted for breakfast
she said
nothing special
I made us scrambled eggs and toast
I put on some coffee
but Candy didn't drink any
I told her we could go see about her car today
I had it towed to the garage
they told me it would be five hundred dollars
something about the distributor
I pulled out my credit card
handed it to the guy behind the counter
for about a month things were good
we went to bed each night and
in the morning Candy gave me her wake-up call
then the shower and breakfast
but once Candy had her car back
she started leaving after we were done eating
telling me she had things to do and

she'd see me later that night
one night when I came home
Candy's car was already in the driveway
when I came into the house
I heard noises coming from the bedroom
I walked back there and
there was Candy on the bed
up on all fours getting fucked from behind
by some guy with long stringy hair
I didn't say anything
just grabbed the guy and
pulled him away from Candy
I threw him to the floor
before kicking him in the balls
I heard him yelp and his dick went limp
like the air being let out of a balloon
the guy started gathering up his clothes
I guess he was a lover not a fighter
Candy started apologizing to me
throwing her arms around me and
rubbing her naked body against my own
but I tore her loose and
pushed her back onto the bed
the lover was already gone
I got Candy's suitcases out
started throwing her stuff into them
she said
wait
let's talk about this
I kept filling up the suitcases
while she followed me around saying
wait wait
when I was done
I took the suitcases to the front door and
threw them outside
then I went and got Candy
she was pulling the sheet from the bed around her
I picked her up and

carried her to the front door
she was still saying *wait*
beating on me with her fists
she lost the sheet and
I pushed her outside
locked the front door
I heard her on the other side
screaming and swearing at me
then she was quiet for a long time
a few minutes later
she knocked on the door
in a calm voice she said
I don't have my keys
I found them in the living room
I opened the door just enough to toss them to her
she had put some clothes on
I heard her car start up
listened to it drive away
I went to the kitchen
pulled some whiskey from
the cupboard above the stove
poured some in a glass
drank it down
poured me some more
there was moonlight coming through the window
a calm permeating the room
I wasn't thinking about Candy
I wasn't going to think about her anymore
I was just sitting there
touching the bottle lightly with my fingers
wondering how long it had been
since I'd gotten really drunk

My 8th Grade Year

I remember wanting to die
after Lisa's cousin rejected me
it meant everything to me
so I went and laid down
in the middle of the road
and all the kids came out to get me
but I ran into the field
where they couldn't find me
I tried to throw dirt at the moon
but wasn't strong enough to reach it
later I walked through the fire
covering my shoes with ashes
it made them all laugh and helped them
forget what had happened

We Laugh About It Now

for some unknown reason
we start arguing and
I get so angry
I want to kill you
we've been drinking
all afternoon and
I run to the kitchen
knocking over the trash and
grab a knife from the drawer
when I enter the living room
waving the knife in the air
you get up and run outside
I chase you into the yard
screaming at the top of my lungs
your girlfriend trailing after me
the sexy blond who
loved to go around topless
she's wearing a red halter
top and cut-off jeans
she says she'll sleep with me
if I just give her the knife
tells me she thinks I'm so
strong and handsome and
it works because I give her
the knife and she kisses me
her tongue swirling in my mouth
we go back in the house and
she sits real close to me
while we have a few more drinks
until I pass out and
the next morning both of
you are gone and
I keep calling your
girlfriend's number all day
long but nobody answers

I Felt the Waves Crashing Over Us

the sky was gray and
her eyes
kept pulling me inside
those deep green pools
where I wanted to drown
I kept swimming around
holding my breath
for as long as I could
until I thought I would explode
before breaking the surface and
coming up for air
holding on to her
never wanting to let her go and
the weight of my body
slipping
I felt the waves
crashing over us and
when I looked at her face
I saw her eyes were closed
I couldn't say anything
but I wanted her to see me
I thought
if she could only see me
then she could save me and
everything would turn out okay

What I Saw

when I drove past
were his shoes sticking out
from beneath the blue tarp
EMTs waiting next to
the ambulance and
the lawnmower silent
against the tree
where it died
after running out of gas

They Say

walking for 30 minutes
at least three times a week
is a good way to stay in shape
but every time I go walking
I start thinking too much
I start wondering about too many things
and I guess that's what happens
living in the same place
where I grew up
all the houses I pass
remind me of something and
I remember the people
who lived there years ago and
it makes me start wondering
whatever happened to them
I try imagining
what they did with their lives and
some of them
I just don't care about
because they never liked me anyway and
then there are the other ones
I wish I could forget
but I keep seeing their faces
even in my dreams

Meat Loaf Amen

I guess I must have been
about seven or eight
the night the preacher
came to our house for supper
my mother had invited him
after church on the previous sunday
when she stood at the door
waiting to leave
complimenting him on
such a fine sermon
I remember it well
because she was squeezing my hand
so I couldn't get loose and
chase after the girls
with all the other boys
I knew my father didn't like it
because I heard my parents
discussing it that night
my father's voice
coming from the living room
why the hell does he have to come here
because
my mother telling him
he's a bachelor and
could probably use a good meal
I was warned to be on
my best behavior and
when the preacher arrived
I didn't say much
but just kept watching him
I'd never seen anybody
eating supper in a suit before
at least not in our house and
he didn't act like
any of my father's friends
I was pretty certain
the preacher wasn't going to

ask me to go get him a beer or
start singing one of those dirty songs
the way they did sometimes
the preacher seemed kind of awkward
like he didn't feel comfortable
outside of the church and
he talked sort of funny
no matter what he said
it sounded like one of his sermons and
when he held up his plate and
asked my mother for
another helping of
her delicious meat loaf
I saw her smile and
lean forward
before she said amen

Waiting Room

flashing lights
through the window
registration desk
people waiting in line
2 Pepsi machines
sitting side by side
coffee vending machine
with
the handwritten sign
Please
Do Not Use
television
on without sound
magazines scattered over
the small table in
the corner all alone
woman wearing sweat pants
talking on her phone
rows of empty chairs
waiting to be filled

Monkey Pile
for Duane May, 1957-2007

when I think about my brother-in-law Duane
one of the things I remember
is his monkey pile story
do you know what monkey pile means?
I think we called it pile-up
when I was a boy
that's when you have a group of boys
and you get somebody on the ground
before shouting pile-up
and then everybody jumps on him
so that he ends up
on the bottom of the pile
but Duane told me
they called it monkey pile
when he was growing up and
he said
he was out somewhere playing
probably in the park
because
he said
they didn't live too far from there
and these boys showed up
and started screaming monkey pile at him
but Duane wasn't going to
let them monkey pile him
so he started running for home
with these boys chasing after him
screaming monkey pile
monkey pile
the whole way there
and when he got there
Duane said
he ran into the house
and told his Dad
there were a bunch of boys outside
and they wanted to monkey pile him

and his Dad said what
so Duane told him what it was
and then his Dad came out and said
they all just needed to leave
and I like remembering that story
because
when I do
it always makes me smile

The Way She Says My Name

I know by the way
she says my name
when I answer the phone
like she's reading it
from the computer screen
in front of her
that it's one of those calls
where I usually hang up
right about this time
but her voice sounds so sexy
as she talks about
credit protection and
identity theft that
I just let her
keep going on and on
imagining her doing
all kinds of
wonderful things to me
saying yes with my eyes closed
when she stops and
asks me if I want it
having no idea
what I've just agreed to do

Better Than Yesterday

I just saw this blackened stump
over in the neighbor's yard and
it looks like a dead horse to me
its head missing and
lying on its back with
its four legs pointing toward the sky and
I wish they'd finish burning it
because I don't want to be
reminded of a dead horse
every time I look over there and
I thought today was going to be
better than yesterday
but I can't shake these feelings
they keep clinging to me
like a second skin and
I keep walking around
feeling like I'm lost again and
never really knowing
what I'm going to find

Black Spiral Notebook

there are several failed plans
for world domination
an elaborate murder plot
lists of things to do
words
I will never have any use for
recipes for foods
no one will ever eat
descriptions of my dreams
to help me remember
long rants against authority
drawings of strange things
I wish really existed
a love poem
for anyone who cares
your name
over and over again

In the Room Where We Hide

you arrive late with
your hair disheveled
and
the light
bursting from your skin
you have touched me
you have broken me open
and
something rises up
from the pieces
darkened wings sweeping over me
when I'm sleeping
and
dreaming
something into awakening
clutching it in my hands
feeling your dark beauty
pressing against my body
in the room where we hide
and
there's never enough time

Getting Offers In the Mail for Gay Porn

glancing at the envelope
I think it's for
the other kind of porn
until I open it
and see pictures of men
rubbing against other men
I prefer looking at women
but it doesn't disgust me
like it might some other guys
hell
to each his own
I say
thinking about this guy
I used to work with years ago
how he went ballistic
any time you joked around with him
about anything
having to do with being gay
he said
they ruined a perfectly good word
and of course
that just made us
tease him even more
when I get up and
throw the whole thing in the trash
on top of the old coffee filters
and yesterday's broken chicken bones
I wonder
how my name and address
ended up on their list
I mean— what?
just because I'm in my 40s
and have never been married
that automatically makes me gay?
it kind of reminds me
of being back in high school
when they called you a faggot

because of
how your voice sounded
or the way you ran during PE
as if
any of those things
had anything to do with it

Marissa

she looks so beautiful
whenever I see her
it makes me shiver inside
she probably thinks
I'm stalking her
the way I show up
every morning and
take one of the tables
lining the back wall
she gets Wednesdays off
unless they need her
to fill in for someone else
I bring my notebook with me
and a pen
sometimes
I wish she'd ask me
what I'm writing about
because
I'd like to tell her something
but she never does
when she glides over
and asks me what I want
her smile's full of sunlight
name tag crooked
across the front of her uniform
I take a quick glance
then look away
afraid of my eyes
lingering there for too long

Dark Red Plastic

yesterday
I noticed the bottle of shampoo
she left behind in the bathroom
the kind I never use and
it stood there on the shelf
dark red plastic
glaring back at me
I should throw it away
remembering
the sweet smell of her hair
brushing against my face
the vision of her
emerging from the shower
her body so smooth
glistening in the light

Where Babies Come From

I don't think I ever asked
my parents about it
so I don't know
what they would've told me
but I don't think
they would've said anything about
storks or cabbage leaves
because
we were way past all that
and
I remember hearing the word
fuck
for the first time in
the second grade
the kid who'd been held back
from the year before
telling several of us one day
on the playground
and
years later in high school
I sat in health class
listening to the teacher
talk about vaginas
while I stared at the pretty girl
sitting across the room
and
those TV shows and movies
when the wide-eyed child
approaches the parents
and asks them nonchalantly
where babies come from
and the parents smile
exchanging knowing glances
with one another before
one of them says
well
when a mommy and
a daddy love each other…

as if love has
everything to do with it
the countless broken homes
with other stories to tell
and
I realize
it doesn't really matter
we need to shift our focus
and not worry so much about
where babies come from
but
what happens to them
where they end up
the kind of people
they will eventually become

The War on TV

I was halfway through a pizza
when they launched the first missiles
it must have been
night time over there
because
I remember
watching streaks of light
flashing on the screen
I kept reminding myself
this was real and
somewhere
people were dying
but it was easy to forget
because
they never showed us the bodies
I remember
going to the kitchen and
getting myself another beer
before I came back and
grabbed another slice
I sat there
holding the remote
waiting to see
what would happen next

Boys

they find something
fluttering in the bushes
something strange and
they poke it
with their sticks
provoking it
until it emerges and
they don't know what it is
they clutch it in
their fumbling hands
laughing at the heart beating
desperate to escape
they pull off the wings
so it can no longer fly
smash it
beneath their feet
curl their fingers into guns
kill each other
over and over again

This Morning I Remember My Father

this is how it usually happens
some piece of a conversation
comes back to me
when I'm doing something
completely unrelated and
this morning
I remember my father
telling me about
some school play he was in and
years later
I remember him
reciting his only line
"I hit the nail on the head
but it was my thumbnail"
we were probably sitting
out there in the back yard
underneath the apple trees
because
that's where my father
liked to go in the afternoons
walking with his cane
through the grass
his radio in the pocket of his shirt

Friday Night Fish Fry Down at the Legion Hall

the old veterans get drunk
but they never talk about the war
they laugh and joke with each other
sharing stories about their children
and grandchildren
and some of the good times
they remember from their youth
the young veterans sit around
they like listening to their stories
they say things are different now
but in a lot of ways they're still the same
the old veterans get into friendly arguments
until their wives come along
and tell them
it's time for them to leave
the young veterans linger in the parking lot
they're not ready to go to sleep
they stand around smoking cigarettes
talking about cars and sports
and what's good on TV
they make plans to get together
again real soon
then somebody asks about Joe
has anybody seen him lately
wonder how he's doing these days
I thought he said he was going to
come over and see us this week

It's Only a Paper Moon

in the photograph my grandfather's
wearing a suit and tie
cap pushed back from his forehead
his thick brown hair
parted down the middle and
he's young and alone
sitting on the moon
white stars stuck on
the dark cloth behind him
the sign above his head
"won't go home 'till morning"
it makes me think of the song
It's Only A Paper Moon
I looked it up on the internet
I remember the movie
Paper Moon with Ryan O'Neal
and his daughter Tatum
the youngest person to
ever win an Oscar
the song was written in 1933
by Harold Arlen
with lyrics by E.Y. Harburg
and Billy Rose
I don't know if my grandfather
was familiar with the song
but I like to imagine him
singing it to my grandmother
at night
when they were all alone
maybe
he took her in his arms
and danced her around the room
singing
"it's only a paper moon
sailing on a cardboard sea"
while my grandmother laughed
with her head thrown back

and her eyes closed
I don't think my grandfather
knew anything about the movie
but I can't be sure
because
it was released
the year before he died

Union 76 Truckstop, After 2 am

we're on our way home
drunk and hungry so we
stop for a patty melt and fries
take our seats in the booth
in the area marked for
professional drivers only but
nobody makes us move
while we're eating the waitress
brings us a note
says it's from the two women
sitting over there and
she points to the booth on
the opposite wall but
from where I'm sitting
I can't see anything
but Gus can and
I ask him what they look like
but he crumples the note and
throws it on the table with
our growing pile of
wadded-up napkins and says
you don't want to know

Trying to Write My Own Love Song

some nights
I walked over to the bar
where I heard people laughing and
having a good time
I ordered a beer and
started looking around
but I never found anyone
just sat there drinking
with the laughter and the music
floating up around me
like this for hours
until I was good and drunk
and I staggered home
alone
the house flooded with silence
darkness painted like a wall
dividing up all the rooms
I kept a pitcher of water
in the refrigerator and
I stumbled into the kitchen
and got myself a drink
later
when I fell asleep
I must've dreamed of summer and
the air was alive
with the heavy scent of flowers
but that was a long time ago
when I was still young and
trying to write my own love song
something with a good beat
but you couldn't really dance to it

He'll Feel It in the Morning

there were these red-carpeted stairs you had
to climb in order to get to the bar
downstairs was where the strip club was located
but we didn't go there
we just walked on up to the bar
and when we reached the top of the stairs
a guy walking the other way suddenly
lost his footing and tumbled down them
falling all the way to the bottom
before coming to a stop
and then he stood up as if nothing
had happened and continued on his way

Getting Old

found a porn mag abandoned
at the side of the road
the cover missing
pages wrinkled and
nearly 20 years old
but nothing much had changed and
I wondered how long
it had laid there
the cars passing by and
some teenager probably tossed it
after showing it to his friends
laughing about how he got it
the other night from his father's
secret stash hidden in
the back of his parents' closet
or maybe some guy just decided
it was time to clean out his car
and found it buried under the front seat
beneath old napkins and
fast-food wrappers and
threw it out for me to find
flipping through the pages
letting the car idle while
watching for somebody's approach
before giving it back to the ditch
driving away thinking
I'm really getting old

Everybody Needs a Dream

he's got hundreds of
ketchup packets stashed in
his apartment
says he always grabs
a few extra ones
every time he goes out to eat
that way he never has to buy
any of his own ketchup
he's got some napkins and
mustard packets but mostly it's
the ketchup packets he keeps
he tells me with all the money
he's saving not having to
buy ketchup he might get a
big-screen TV and I watch him
for another moment as he
gets really excited telling me
maybe he'll buy himself a car
but you don't drive I say
yeah he says but with all the money
he can hire someone
to drive him around
then he asks me if I want to
go with him to get
something to eat
he says just think
the more I eat out
the more ketchup I get and
the more money I save
I start to say something
but decide to let it go because
everybody needs a dream and
I'm not going to be
the son of a bitch who
ruins it for him

Pieces

one night she came over and
brought a jigsaw puzzle with her
so we could work on it together
she told me
while I poured some whiskey
into big glasses of Coke
after we got started
we discovered
some of the pieces were missing
but she couldn't remember
where she lost them and
then she started thinking about
where she got the puzzle from
in the first place
but couldn't come up
with a good answer
I told her it was okay
it didn't really matter
because we were drinking and
having a good time and
I started kissing her
pulling her head toward me and
every time I touched her lips
she laughed
I said
we can make our own puzzle pieces
but it was probably
just the whiskey talking
but it didn't stop me
from pulling out some old pictures
I dug out of a kitchen drawer
my father
I said
holding up one of the photos
she said
he looks just like you
I told her she was drunk

before taking a pair of scissors to
some of the pictures
cutting them to fit into
the puzzle's empty spaces
I like it better this way
I said
taking a drink from my glass
so do I
she said
before I grabbed her again
holding my mouth against hers
even when she started to laugh

The Phone Dials Your Number

been driving around for awhile
before I think about you
picking up the cell phone
from the passenger's seat
I find your name among
my list of contacts
push the button and
the phone dials your number
hearing the first ring
I turn down the radio
keeping my eyes on the road
another ring and then
your voice says, hello, and
I ask you what you're doing
your voice says, nothing, like
you're not sure and
I'm making a right turn
wondering how many miles
away from me you are
I start to say something
but the sound beeps in my ear and
just like that you're gone
I'm alone
call was lost
flashing on the screen

Flashes of Light

coming back to this house
again
after you were gone and
the rooms had been changed and
I kept seeing things
these random flashes of light and
maybe
I went crazy for awhile
this flickering of the screen
like a movie playing and
the night of your visitation
we drove to the funeral home
located in another town and
as soon as I saw it
I knew
that wasn't you anymore
just the body dressed up
pretending to be you
lying there and
I didn't say anything
you were probably somewhere
laughing at us
because of how funny
we must have looked
sitting there
like we didn't know what to do

Another Sunday Morning Hangover

I don't know why
I keep doing this to myself
I guess a man
has to do something
with his time and
it sure beats sitting around
feeling stone cold sober
on a lonely saturday night
staring at the walls and
why the hell does my neighbor
find it necessary
to keep revving the engine
of his pick-up truck
hell
doesn't he know
his driveway's not too far
from my bedroom window and
there's a bad taste in my mouth
like I swallowed a dirty pillow and
it's stuck in my throat and
it won't dissolve
I really need to take a piss
but my legs hurt and
maybe
I overdid it again
last night
like I always do
but there's sunlight
screaming through the windows and
goddamn
it feels good to be alive

I Keep Coming

into the living room
and looking out the window
thinking I'm going to see
somebody
I haven't seen for a long time
pulling into my driveway
but there's nobody out there
so I go into the kitchen
and grab myself another beer
my fourth one so far
and that's after the three
whiskey and Cokes
I drank at
the beginning of the night
I mean
you know what they say
beer before hard
you're out in the yard
hard before beer
and you're in the clear
words
I try to live by and
I like to count my beers
lining the bottles up
across the kitchen table
so I can see how it's going
something I like to do
when I'm trying to get drunk

Applebees, Cold Thursday Night

they're sitting at the table across from me
and I can't help overhearing them
two pretty blondes not more than
seventeen or eighteen and one of them
mentions something about divorce as
the other one gazes silently into her plate
the air turning somber above the uneaten
remains of their appetizer tray and
I take another drink of my beer
waiting to hear more but they
start eating again and giggling over
some secret shared between themselves
and I drink from my beer suddenly struck
by the notion of wanting to buy their dinner
and for the rest of the evening as I finish
my boneless buffalo wings can't think of
anything else wanting to tell the waiter
to put their bill on my credit card and
not to mention my name because it thrilled me
to think about them sitting there finished
with their meal and the waiter telling them
the check had been taken care of and
I didn't want anything from them
just wanted to leave an impression
something they could always talk about
imagining them later saying to each other
remember the time we went to Applebees
and somebody paid for our dinner

Plastic Cowboy

I had a plastic horse
with a plastic saddle molded
on its back and plastic
wheels under each hoof
when I sat on it and
bounced up and down
the horse moved across the floor
and I wore a plastic cowboy hat
with a matching plastic badge
and a plastic vest made to
look as if it were leather
and my plastic holster held
my plastic gun and bullets
and I rode through the house
looking for outlaws playing
quick draw and shouting bang
whenever I found their hiding places
but when I grew older
I gathered up my plastic
cowboy gear except for
the horse which I no longer had
and took it out behind the garage
where no one could see me and
set it all on fire
watching as it melted into a
large gooey puddle and
thick black smoke choked
the bright blue sky

Because

she's a beautiful woman
I can't stop thinking about her
she's a beautiful woman and
I have trouble sleeping at night
I keep getting drunk
because
she doesn't want to be with me
but when I see her smile
while I'm hiding in the shadows
I hear the sound of
a million birds taking flight
she's a beautiful woman and
my heart breaks
because
she doesn't want to
get to know me better
I know
I should just forget her and
try to move on
but I don't think I can
because
she's a beautiful woman and
I keep thinking
maybe
some day
I can change her mind

Walking Home Drunk Again

and when I pass the yellow house on
the corner where the young blonde lives
I start slowing down to
glance up at the windows
hoping to catch a glimpse of her
but they're all dark and
everybody's asleep so
I take out pen and paper
decide to write her a note
scribbling some words in the darkness
thinking they're the most beautiful
words anyone's ever written but
I'm afraid to sign my name so
instead I write *from somebody you know*
before sticking it under
the windshield wiper of
the car sitting near the road
like I'm giving out a parking ticket
then I stumble on home

Teacher

yes
she was my teacher
almost 30 years ago
I just read it in the paper
she's a grandmother now
but I keep seeing her in my mind
still young and beautiful and
I remember how all the boys
were in love with her
how she always wore those
short skirts and
we'd drop our pencils
whenever she came near us
so we could peek up her dress and
we'd raise our hands
when we were working on
something in class so
she'd stroll over to us and
bring her face really close to ours
giving us a chance to
see down the front of her blouse and
I can't help but laugh about it now
I wonder if she ever suspected
what we were doing and
if she still teaches anywhere

The Night My Brother Died

I was dreaming about my grandmother
from my mother's side of the family
I never really knew her
she died when I was three and
the only image I remember is
seeing her lying in bed with her back to me
I'm not sure it's a real memory
or something I just made up
but does it really matter and
what does it have to do with my brother dying

the night my brother died
my mother's voice woke me
she was crying and
telling me to come downstairs
I felt something in my stomach tighten
when I started my descent
toward the light
coming from the kitchen

the night my brother died is
more than twenty years in the past and
I'm still trying to figure it out
but sometimes people just die and
there's no meaning behind it
I know it's hard to accept that
because I keep yearning for closure
I want to go somewhere and
find some kind of peace but
maybe I'll just get drunk tonight and
try to forget for a little while
come back tomorrow and
start again

Light Comes Through the Window

every morning
when I awaken
I feel the struggle begin
every morning
when the sun rises and
the light comes through the window
I try to think of a reason
why I should get out of bed
sometimes
I'm reminded of the past and
the soft laughter
of a beautiful woman
sometimes
I remember
the comfort that comes
from drunkenness
before I roll over
slowly
turning off the alarm
because
it's almost time and
I hate the way it sounds

This Morning Over the Phone

my mom mentions something about
the dream she had last night
telling me
how she doesn't like dreaming
about people who are dead
and I don't think to ask her
why this bothers her so much
and I don't tell her about
how I dream about
the dead all the time
mostly my father
and my brother
and sometimes
my uncle
who used to stay with us
most of the time
they never really do anything
they're just there with me
in the same rooms
looking pretty much like
how I remember them
before I awaken
and they're almost alive

I Don't Know What I Want

stopping at the gas station
on my way home
filling the tank and
running up the total to
an even dollar amount
after the nozzle shuts off
when I go inside to pay
I walk around looking over
all the junk food on display
but nothing sounds good to me
finally settling on
the large bottle of soda
the oversized candy bar
not really wanting them
but feeling the need to
buy something besides the gas

The Neighbor's Daughter

a couple of months ago
she started coming home
on the weekends
I think she goes to college
some school far away from here
maybe
in another state
I'm not sure

I don't know what she's studying
I never really talked to her
we've only exchanged occasional greetings
when both of us happened to be
outside at the same time and
she always flashes me
with this beautiful smile

sometimes I see her
just coming and going
watching her through
my living room window
traipsing across the yard
her thick red hair
sweeping past her shoulders and
cascading softly down her back

not too long ago I saw her
out there in the driveway
washing her car in
the afternoon sun
she was wearing this pair of
little short shorts and
when she bent over
her shirt kept riding up
revealing part of her lower back and
what looked to me
like a butterfly tattoo

just this small area of flesh
less than what you'd see
if she had been at the beach
but for some reason
I thought it was wonderful

I Wanted to Know Her Name

I watched her through the window
getting out of the car
she stood on the sidewalk
finishing her cigarette
she was wearing denim shorts and
a bright red tube top
I wanted to know her name
but I was too afraid to ask
when she walked past me
she caught me staring
but all she did was smile
I felt warm
I picked up my glass and
took a long drink
then
the waitress came over
and asked me
if I wanted some dessert

Cruel Summer

it was a cruel summer
if you don't believe me
just go ask
the women from Bananarama
see what they're doing now
maybe
if you ask them nicely
they'll perform
their remake of Venus for you
I use to masturbate
while watching their videos
I think one of them
married Dave Stewart
from the band Eurythmics
I wonder if they're still together
does anybody here know
whatever happened to Annie Lennox
she frightened me
the first time I saw her
in the video for Sweet Dreams
late-night Friday
on cable TV and
I never had any plans for the weekend
I usually just slept in late

When I Speak Your Name

I don't remember the sound
of your voice
your photograph stares
back at me and
reminds me of what
you must have looked like
but every year
you seem less real to me
like some dream-image
floating up from
the darkness of my childhood and
when I speak your name
I struggle with meaning
as if I truly believe
you never existed and
it was me who
conjured you
up from the dust
and there's nothing for which
I need to be forgiven

The Sound of His Voice

it's gone now and
I can never get it back
the sound of his voice
when he called my name
from the bottom of the stairs
the sound of his voice
when he answered the phone and
I don't remember it
anymore
all I have are these photographs
full of ugly silences and
moments frozen in time
they can't help me now
reminders of what he looked like
the sound of his voice
when he said he was sorry
lost in the vacuum of time

The Good Life

he claimed
he brought a case of beer
home every night and
drank until he passed out
he prided himself on
never being late to work
when I heard him
he was giving it to the younger guys
he told them
hangovers were nothing
but a state of mind and
he laughed and said
they should always try to
drink plenty of water
he'd been with the company
for 20 years and
everybody seemed to like him
he started here
just a couple of years after high school
he tried going to college
but he said it didn't take
on weekends he drank whiskey
he said
he liked it mixed with Mountain Dew
whenever he got a new woman
he'd go around talking about her
but when anybody asked him
if he was going to settle down
he swore to them
he was never getting married
one day
during afternoon break
somebody asked him
what he'd do if he ever
ended up winning the lottery and
he started laughing
threw his hands up and said

no thanks
he didn't want that kind of money
too much to worry about
he told us
that was one headache he didn't need

Sometimes I Wish I Could Do It Again

recently I found myself
reminiscing about some of the toys
I had when I was a child
I remember
an orange Tonka dump truck
a metal one
with a real hydraulic cylinder
and how beat up it got
because I took it outside
and played with it in the rocks
I had matchbox cars
and they got all scratched up
because I use to crash them
into each other all the time
I think I ended up
giving them to one of my nephews
I remember
I had an electric train set
actually more than one
I always wanted to set it up
put it on a piece of plywood
and make a whole town out of it
with buildings and trees and people
but for some reason I never did
one of my favorite things
was the plastic cowboys and indians
they came in a bag and
they were all different colors
I remember
how me and my nephew
who was only four years younger than me
would build these elaborate forts
and we'd set up our men
he'd be on one side of the room
and I'd be on the other
then we'd take this little plastic block
and throw it back and forth

trying to knock down
the other person's men
if your men got knocked down
that meant they were dead and
you tried to be the first one
to kill all the other person's men
I remember
after somebody had won
we'd rebuild our forts
and set up our men
then do it all again and
I remember
how we played that way for hours

I Felt Her Body Shiver

ran into one of my old
girlfriends the other day
she looked really good and
I suggested
we go have a drink
after several of them
we made it back to my place
I was feeling good
so I told her
maybe
she should think about
spending the night with me
she laughed
but I could tell she was interested
I said
I've learned a few things
since the last time we were together
she said
well
I wouldn't be surprised
I grabbed her and kissed her
before she had the chance
to say another word
I ran my hand
down the front of her jeans
felt her getting wet
her tongue started snaking
in and out of my mouth
I guided her toward the bedroom
I told her
I wanted to undress her
something
she never let me do before
she always got undressed and
climbed into bed
before I even got in the room
maybe

she was self-conscious about her body
but she had no reason to be
I sat her down
on the edge of the bed and
told her I wanted to
slowly take off her clothes
one piece at a time
I told her
I wanted to expose her
because
she was so beautiful
she blushed and nodded
both at the same time
she pulled me down for another kiss
when we separated
I smiled and
brushed my fingers
delicately across her throat
I felt her body shiver
then I began

Driving Home

near Lotus Road entering
McLean County and I'm
thinking about the girl
the one from the music store
the one with the beautiful face
and the long dark hair
and when she looked at me
I believed she could
see right through me and
shivers running down my back
and I'm passing the road
that goes into Bellflower
heading west on 136 and
I wish things were different
but they're always the same
and I'm driving back home
past the white house with
the candles burning in every window
and I'm thinking about the girl
the one from the music store
the one who doesn't have a name
but her face returns to me
over and over in my dreams and
Heyworth's behind me now
with McLean looming up ahead
I can see the lights from
the Dixie Truckers Home and
I'm almost there
just a few more miles of
darkness to go and the girl
from the music store laughs as
I'm turning on the Stanford road
but when I reach my dark
and empty house she
doesn't make a sound

How Often Do You See Them

I saw a hearse today
heading west
toward the river
when I was coming from the north
heading south
slowing down for the stop sign
the hearse didn't have to stop and
there were two pick-up trucks behind it
one of them was red
but I don't remember
the color of the other one
I don't think they had
anything to do with the hearse
but I don't know that for sure
I guess it was strange
seeing it like that
moving along with
the normal flow of traffic
I mean
how often do you see them
unless they're leading a funeral procession
I kept wondering
if there was a body in the back
or maybe
someone had just died and
it was going to pick them up

The Tuba Player

she was really young
the first time I saw her
and it made me feel old
it made me feel like
I'd missed out on something
when I saw the light
shining down on her
from above and
I knew
it was only the lights
mounted in the ceiling
but it still made her look divine
her blonde hair catching the light
her beauty reflected in
the polished surface of
the tuba as she played
classical music pieces
on a sunday afternoon
during the chill of winter
but not too far
from the beginning of spring

Blue Toenails

I slammed the door on purpose
because
I wanted to let her know I was there
I found her in the bedroom
sitting on the edge of the bed
I noticed
she wasn't wearing any shoes and
her toenails were painted blue
I told her
I was here to get
the rest of my stuff and
she just nodded her head
I only had a couple of bags and
the cardboard box in the hallway
I'd sealed up with duct tape
earlier in the week
I carried the bags out to the car and
when I came back for the box
I heard her saying something
but couldn't understand what it was
I went back to the bedroom and
asked her what she wanted
she looked up and
I could tell she'd been crying
she said
you have some mail
on the kitchen table and
I went to see what it was
just a couple of bills
with my name on them and
some damn credit card offer
advertising
the lowest interest rate around
I heard the faucet dripping and
walked over to the sink and shut it off
remembering
how she was never strong enough

to tighten it until it stopped
I looked out the window
at the back yard and noticed
the grass needed mowing
saw all the sticks scattered on the ground
I thought about
all those dead limbs in the trees
I was going to cut
but never got around to doing
I took the letters and
set them on the box
before I picked it up and
carried it to the front door

Toward the End

what about that night in
the parking lot of Target
when we sat in your car
with the engine running
because
it was cold outside and
you didn't want to leave and
I didn't want to let you go
I kept pressing
my body against you
kissing you every time
I said
you should probably get going and
that was a long ways
from where I am now
at least
it feels like it and
maybe
I should've done
some things differently
but I remember
toward the end
every time I asked you
you told me
it wasn't my fault

The Sound of Machines

my mother's been in the hospital
for over two weeks now
ever since she fell at home
now they're telling us
she needs a pacemaker
and she's been fighting pneumonia
over the past couple of days
having to be on oxygen
wearing a heart monitor and
I know she must be tired
by the way she keeps closing her eyes
I hold on to her hand
and tell her
she should try and
get some sleep and
maybe
that would make her feel better
but she says
she doesn't want to sleep
because
if she does she's afraid
she might not wake up again
and what can I say to her
when she starts talking like that
how can I look at her
lying there in bed
with the sound of machines
surrounding us
and tell her
everything's
going to be okay

Peach Schnapps and Sprite

tonight I'm drinking
peach schnapps and Sprite
like I did
during that party long ago
sitting here
thinking about you
I remember
that was the night
I kissed you
for the first time
and you pushed me away
telling me
you just wanted to be friends
and I said okay
then I got drunk and
acted like an asshole
before stumbling out the back door
without telling you goodbye

The Smell of Burning Leaves

I recognized her
when I saw her coming toward me
walking slowly across the yard
I hadn't seen her for a long time
but she looked about the same to me
just a little older around the eyes
with a sprinkle of gray in her hair
I'd read about her son's death
a couple of days ago in the paper
he was serving in the military and
wouldn't be coming back home
what are you up to
she said
I saw the trace of a smile on her face
I said
just trying to get the yard cleaned up
you know
burning some leaves
I saw her glance at the fire
I said
I'm sorry about your son
because I didn't know what else to say
she looked at the ground
Keith loved the smell of burning leaves
she said
she looked at the fire again
she said
he always did
even when he was little
I looked at the pile of leaves near my feet
at the trash can I was using to
carry the leaves over to the fire
I said
yeah me too
but it sounded really dumb
she touched my arm
but only for a second

I said
so how are you doing
she closed her eyes before answering
as good as I can be
she said
I said
that's all we can do
isn't it
the wind suddenly shifted and
the smoke from the burning leaves
drifted toward us
we wallowed in the silence for several moments
she said
well
I'll let you get back to work
I just saw you out here
and thought I'd come say hello
I said
I'm glad you did
she stepped toward me and
gave me a hug
I said
take care of yourself
when she pulled herself away from me
she said
I have to
and I watched her walk away
but then she stopped and
turned back toward me and
gave me a wave
I waved back at her
before I picked up the trash can and
started dumping more leaves on the fire

Windmills In the Rain

last night
the guy on the news
kept talking about wind farms and
the benefits of finding
alternative sources of energy
he kept referring to them
as wind turbines and
I know
that's what they really are
but I like calling them windmills
because
it sounds more romantic to me
something you want to go see
driving with your lover
huddled close to you
in the front seat of the car
but I'm out here driving around
because
I don't want to go home
there's too much restlessness
running through my brain
something unsettled left inside me and
I can see them
through the rain-streaked windshield
rising up against the leaden sky
their rotors slowly spinning
while others stand motionless
waiting for some invisible signal
to come and turn them on

First Time

I stole a bottle of
vodka from the filing
cabinet in my
parents' bedroom and
brought it to
the party where
I mixed it with
rum and something I
don't remember now
having no idea how
it would send me
early in the night to
the bathroom vomiting
wallowing on the dirty floor
calling some girl's name

The Boy with the Plastic Telephone

they say
it's me in
the photo
age three
or four
the boy
sitting on
the floor
plastic telephone
beside him and
I imagine him
calling Daddy
getting no answer
pondering
the numbers
before dialing again
perhaps he
calls the future
and I answer
as I am now
trying to warn him
but the connection
gets lost
the static swallows
the words and
reminds me
again that I
cannot change
the past

Two Sisters

they moved
into the house
next door
where they
stayed for
one summer
between my
seventh and eighth
grade years
two sisters
one older
one younger
and me
caught in
the middle
not sure
which way
I wanted
to turn
at night
dreaming and
waking
suddenly to
the strange
slickness of
my own skin

Empty Chair

an empty chair could mean
almost anything
an abundance of riches and
you have more chairs than you can use
somebody had to go to the bathroom
it happens
maybe they're just out on the town
having a good time and
they won't be home until late
maybe it's where the children used to sit
but they've all gone away
the death of someone close to you
or maybe the departure of
somebody you thought you knew
but one day they suddenly changed and
you didn't recognize them anymore
because nobody ever sits there and
you can't remember why

James Babbs was born in 1966 and lives in Stanford, Illinois where he earns his living as a rural mail carrier. Over the last 30 years, he has published hundreds of poems in both print and online journals. He is the author of *Dictionary of Chaos* (2002) and *Another Beautiful Night* (2010).

The author gratefully acknowledges the following publications where some of these poems first appeared.

Abbey
Barbaric Yawp
The Beat
Camel Saloon
Chiron Review
decomP
Deuce Coupe
Fight These Bastards
Free Verse
Green Rock
Gutter Eloquence
Indite Circle
Main Street Rag
Mastodon Dentist
Meat Heads and Muscle Cars
My Favorite Bullet
Naked Knuckle
Nerve Cowboy
Opium Poetry
The Panulaan Review
Poetry East
Red Fez
Remark
Snow Monkey
Thieves Jargon
Underground Voices
Verse Wisconsin
Word Riot
Zillah
Zygote In My Coffee
ZYX

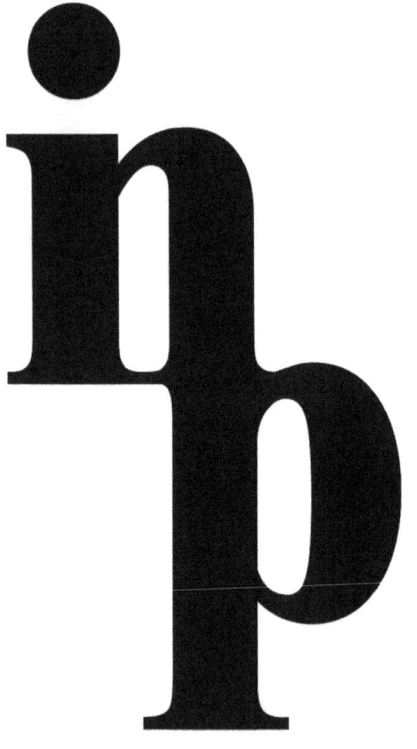

www.interiornoisepress.com

www.ingramcontent.com/pod-product-compliance
Lightning Source LLC
Chambersburg PA
CBHW020936090426

42736CB00010B/1162